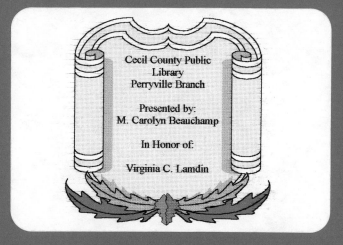

A QUINTET BOOK

Published by Chartwell Books
A Division of Book Sales, Inc.
PO Box 7100
Edison, New Jersey 08818-7100

This edition produced for sale
in the U.S.A., its territories
and dependencies only.

ISBN 0-7858-0314-9

This book was designed and produced by
Quintet Publishing Limited
6 Blundell Street
London N7 9BH

Creative Director: Richard Dewing
Designer: James Lawrence
Project Editor: Claire Tennant-Scull
Editor: Lydia Darbyshire
Photographer: Andrew Sydenham

Typeset in Great Britain by
Central Southern Typesetters, Eastbourne
Manufactured in Singapore by Eray Scan Pte Ltd
Printed in China by Leefung-Asco Printers Ltd

START-A-CRAFT

Mask Making

Get started in a new craft with easy-to-follow

projects for beginners

GILL DICKINSON

CHARTWELL
BOOKS, INC

CONTENTS

INTRODUCTION

As long as people have lived on earth, costumes and masks have been made in some form, either for decoration or for ceremonial or religious purposes. Masks have been used for dance, theater, carnivals, celebrations, pagan and religious rituals – or sometimes just for fun and disguise.

The ancient Greeks were the first to use masks for theatrical performances, and the actors and members of the chorus wore large masks with stylized expressions that could be clearly seen and understood by the audience. We still see traces of these masks in some theaters, which use the outlines of the masks with smiling or sad faces to decorate programs and foyers. Masks were worn by tribal peoples in West Africa to indicate social position, and the Kalahari tribe made ugly masks to drive away demons. Dragon masks are still used to ward off evil spirits in China.

Carnival is a Christian festival that used to take place in many countries before Lent. Elaborate and beautiful masks and costumes were made for this event, especially in the Caribbean and some South American countries. Venetian masks of the kind inspired in the 16th century by Commedia dell'Arte are still seen today. These simple, traditional masks often take the form of elements such as stars, suns, and moons, and half-masks representing characters such as Pierrot, Columbine, and Harlequin are used not only in Italy, where they originated, but all around the world.

Whatever form a mask takes, it acts as a disguise. The wearer can act the fool without being recognized or just simply enjoy being another person. In the 18th century, for example, elegant ladies carried masks so that they could flirt with strangers with impunity. Masks can be used today to conjure of an element of menace, mystery, or fun.

Even a simple half-mask, quickly made and decorated, can be amusing and fun to wear, while more complicated masks can be used for costume parties or for theatrical performances.

The instructions to make 12 exciting masks are given in this book. They range from the simple to the complicated, from half-masks to full masks that completely cover the face. A variety of media have been used, from papier-mâché, fur fabric, and feathers to simple masks made from paper plates, while the Monster mask is made from recycled egg cartons. Many of the masks are decorated with pastels or ordinary paints.

MATERIALS AND TECHNIQUES

PAPER AND CARDBOARD

Paper is a wonderfully versatile product – it is strong enough to be folded and pleated, but it can be torn and cut and then colored and decorated in dozens of ways. You can also obtain paper and cardboard in a variety of weights and colors.

Paper masks are especially easy for young children to make, and they can be as simple or as complicated as you wish. The Seaside Shades are an instant, fun disguise made with paper and glue. Paper plates are available in supermarkets and stationery stores and can be used to make good, strong masks that are light and easy to wear. Decorate them imaginatively; children can do this for themselves using different types of paint and paper.

You can also achieve interesting effects by using colored paper imaginatively to give a fullness and three-dimensional quality to a mask. The mane of the Lion Mask, for instance, is made from thin strips of paper in a variety of shades. Some of the strips are curled with scissors, while others left straight to create an unusually textured, full effect.

PASTEL AND PAINT TECHNIQUES

Although paper and cardboard are available in a wide choice of colors and patterns, there will be times when you want to decorate the surface of the mask in a particular way. We have used either poster paints or pastels for the masks described here.

Pastels are used for the Lion Mask and the basic Half-mask. It is best to experiment with pastels on scrap paper to get a feel for how they work. Try using different colors together and try not to apply them too heavily. They will blend more easily if they are used lightly, and you can merge the colors together by rubbing them gently with a finger to create all kinds of shades and textures very quickly. When you use pastels, it is a good idea to place a clean sheet of paper over areas that you have already colored so that you do not smudge the pastels with your hand. You should always use fixative with pastels, which are not stable and quickly smudge and fade.

Poster paints are widely available, and they are ideal for children to use. Colors can be mixed on saucers or in old food containers.

You can use all kinds of painting techniques on the masks. Spattering with a brush and old toothbrush was used on the Medusa Mask, for example, and you could also use sponges, rags, and, of course, your fingers. For a really rich, deep color, apply one coat and leave it to dry before you apply a second, or even a third, coat.

PAPIER-MÂCHÉ

Making and using papier-mâché is both simple and cheap, but it does need more time, because you have to leave the layers to dry out. When it is finished, papier-mâché is very light but durable, and it will withstand quite a lot of hard wear. It is a very versatile medium, which we have used to make the Punk Mask, which shows how easy it is to build up a quite complex shape. The Witch is the most time-consuming mask in the book, and it is a project for the real enthusiast, although you could cut the time in half by buying a cheap witch's hat from a craft store and decorating it.

Once you have made a papier mâché-mask or half-mask, you can adapt it to all kinds of styles. The Woodland Half-mask could be adapted for different projects, for example – perhaps to look like an animal or even a simple painted Venetian-style mask. Making papier-mâché can be a rather messy process, so remember to cover your work surface with newspaper before you begin. Use either ordinary newspaper or lightweight paper to make papier-mâché.

The Layering Method

◊ Tear the strips of paper into fairly small, even-sized pieces.

◊ Mix a smooth paste from flour and water or use a commercial wallpaper paste or a weak solution of white craft glue.

◊ So that you can be sure that you have completely covered the mask with each layer, either use different colors for each layer or lay the strips in different directions each time.

◊ Make sure that the previous layer is completely dry before you begin to apply the next layer.

◊ Do not put papier-mâché near a radiator or in front of a fire to dry – the paper will crack and twist out of shape. Leave it in a warm, dry room for about 2 hours.

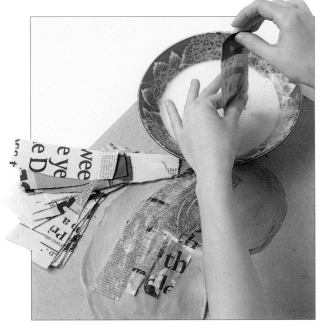

The Pulp Method

Some of the masks – the Witch and the Punk, for example – involve the use of papier-mâché pulp to build up the features. You can buy pulp in many craft stores, but it is quite easy and much cheaper to make your own, especially as you will need only small amounts at a time.

◊ Tear newspaper into small pieces.

◊ Mix some paste and immerse the torn paper in it. Make sure all the pieces of paper are covered in the paste, but do not allow them to become saturated.

◊ Squeeze the paste out of the paper and mold the pulp into shape. It will adhere easily to the surface of papier-mâché.

◊ The pulp will take longer to dry than single layers of papier-mâché, and it is best to leave it overnight if possible to make sure it is absolutely dry.

HOLDING THE MASKS IN PLACE

Elastic can be used to hold masks in place, but some of the more complicated masks, especially the Punk and Witch, need strong tape. Outsize masks, like the Monster, are best secured with strips of cardboard that run over the top and around the back of the head.

◊ The simplest method is to attach ties (either plastic or fabric) to the reverse side of the sides of the mask with strong tape.

◊ Make a small hole at each side of the mask and push string or elastic through the holes. Hold the elastic or string in place by tying neat knots on the right side so that they do not slide through the holes.

◊ Make a slit at each side of the mask and thread the ties through the slits from the back and use tape to hold the ends of the ties securely at the back of the mask. The ties emerge at the front so that they can be taken around to the back of the head and tied together.

◊ Use a small stick – bamboo canes sold in garden centers for propping up plants are ideal – and secure it to the back of the mask with strong tape. This method means that the mask can be raised and lowered easily.

◊ Cut two strips of lightweight cardboard, one to reach around the back of your head, and the second to reach from the top front of the mask to about halfway down your head so that it reaches the first piece. Check that the mask is comfortable and secure before stapling the strips to the edge of the mask and to each other.

FABRIC AND FEATHERS

The Panda Mask is made from fur fabric, which looks wonderfully appealing. Other masks could easily be made from scraps of left-over fabric so that you can use different colors and textures. Fur fabric is available from most craft and fabric stores, and it is easy to work with. There is no need to stitch the pieces together – a clear adhesive or a special fabric adhesive will hold the material firmly together.

Feathers give a wonderfully sophisticated, rather exotic look to a mask. You can buy ready-dyed ones, but it is easy to color feathers with ordinary cold water dye, so you could, for example, make a feathered mask to match a particular dress or outfit. Look in fishing equipment departments for some unusual feathers, as well as in craft suppliers.

Your local craft or fabric store will also be a good source for a variety of beads, sequins, and spangles that can be used in various ways to decorate masks. Even a simple half-mask can be enlivened by an edging of multicolored sequins.

SEASIDE SHADES

This mask is fun to make, and it should be fun to wear. We have used the outline of a fish, but you could use a starfish or crabs, for which we have included templates, or you could design your own glasses, drawing your inspiration from anything you see on the seashore – shells or seaweed, for example. We decorated the mask with self-adhesive dots and colored paper, but you could make it really spectacular by using beads or sequins.

You will need

◊ Medium-weight green cardboard
◊ Pencil
◊ Tracing paper
◊ Scissors
◊ Hole punch
◊ Tape
◊ Colored construction paper
◊ Colored self-adhesive dots
◊ Black felt-tip pen
◊ Clear, all-purpose glue
◊ Pinking shears

1 Trace the image of your choice and the side pieces from the template on page 45 onto medium-weight green cardboard. Punch out the eye holes and cut out the shape and side pieces.

2 Turn over the shape and use tape to attach the side pieces.

3 Decorate the cut-out fins with strips of colored paper and self-adhesive dots. Use a felt-tip pen to make some smaller spots in the center of the dots.

4 Score along the narrow edge of each fin and fold them along the score line. Apply glue to the small flap and glue each fin in place on the front of the mask.

5 Place a small black self-adhesive dot in the center of a large white dot and punch a hole through the center.

6 Place this over one of the eye holes already made. Repeat for the other eye.

7 Cut some curved pieces from a piece of colored paper – we used turquoise – and glue them in position, using the illustration as a guide.

8 Cut some more curved strips in a contrasting color – we used dark blue – and glue them in place, together with some more colored dots. You may find a wooden toothpick useful for pushing and pressing the small dots into place.

9 Cut some wedge-shaped pieces of light blue paper, using pinking shears to give a neatly jagged edge, and glue long triangles of dark blue paper down the center of each piece.

10 Glue these blue pieces to the tails of the fish.

TIP

• You can buy self-adhesive dots – and other shapes – that are already colored, but rather than buy colored ones that you may never use, buy white ones and paint them to match the other colors that you are using on your mask. Apply the paint before you peel the dot away from the backing sheet so that you can paint right up the edges of the circle. If you try to apply the paint once the dot is in place, you will find it difficult to paint it neatly without getting paint on the background color.

11 Finish off with some strips of yellow paper,
cut into long, narrow wedge shapes, and glue them
in position along the top edges of the fish.

HALF-MASK

This striking half-mask is easily made with medium-weight cardboard, and it is colored with pastels. We have included two templates, one for a man (page 48) and one for a woman (page 46), and you can use the basic design and method in many different ways, changing the hairstyle and the hat to give a completely different effect. Look through a library book to get some ideas from historical costumes, especially uniforms.

You will need
◊ Medium-weight cardboard
◊ Pencil
◊ Tracing paper
◊ Scissors
◊ Colored pastels
◊ Fixative
◊ Black crayon
◊ Craft knife
◊ Twill tape
◊ Tape
◊ 2 ostrich feathers

1 Transfer the outline of the template on page 48 to white cardboard and cut around the outline.

2 Take a selection of flesh-colored pastels and begin to shade in the face area. Blend the colors by rubbing them gently with a finger.

TIP

• Half-masks give only a partial disguise because the wearer's mouth and nose are still visible. Try to match the skin color of the mask to the tones of the wearer's own skin.

3 Mark the eyebrows with brown pastel and use darker pink for the areas around the temples. Spray lightly with fixative.

4 Use several shades of brown to color the hair. Color in the hat, using the illustration as a guide.

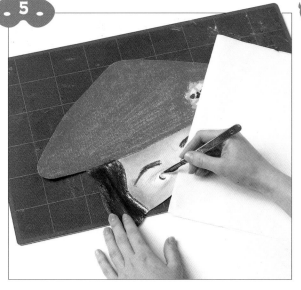

5 Cut out the eye holes with a craft knife, using a piece of spare paper over the mask so that you do not smudge the colors with your hand.

6 Color in the area around the eye holes with black crayon and shade in the darker areas of the face. Finish the hair, lightly smudging the color with your finger, then spray it with fixative.

7 Finish off the hat with random sweeps of orange.

8 Spray the mask with fixative and leave to dry.

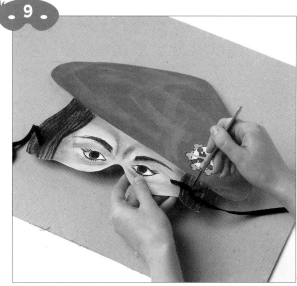

9 Use the craft knife to make tiny slits at the side of the mask in the hair area and push lengths of twill tape through to the back.

TIP

• We used black twill tape to tie on the mask because it is less obvious with dark hair. If you change the hair color, use tape that matches the hair color as closely as possible.

.10.

10 Turn over the mask and secure the twill tape with strong tape.

11 Tape two feathers together and put them in position. Attach them to the back of the mask with strong tape.

.11.

LION MASK

You will need paper, cardboard, and pastels for this mask, which is really fairly simple to make, although it does look very impressive. It is quite time-consuming to complete, because the lion's mane is made from individual strips of paper, and although it would be possible to make a less complicated version – a child could easily make the basic mask – the mane really does bring the mask to life.

You will need
◊ Medium-weight brown cardboard
◊ Pencil
◊ Tracing paper
◊ Scissors
◊ Hole punch
◊ Pastels, including white, shades of brown, and black
◊ Fixative
◊ Black crayon
◊ Medium-weight paper, four shades from brown to beige
◊ Lightweight white paper
◊ Clear, all-purpose glue
◊ Self-adhesive dots, black and yellow
◊ Twill tape or elastic

1 Transfer the outline from the template on page 47 to the brown cardboard and cut out the shape.

2 Cut around the nose area and punch out the eye holes (for you to see through).

3 Use a selection of brown, yellow, and beige pastels to begin to color in and shade the lion's face.

4 Use white to color in around the mouth, eyes, and eyebrows and rub the pastels carefully with your finger to blend the colors together. Spray with fixative and leave to dry.

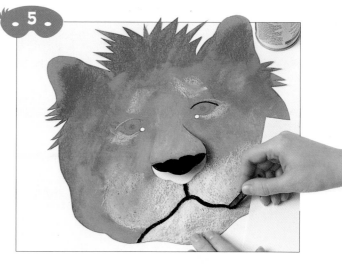

5 Use the black crayon to draw in the line of the mouth and the nostrils.

6 Protect the pastels you have applied by resting your hand on a piece of spare white paper while you work. Draw round the eyes with black crayon.

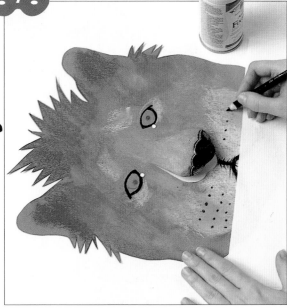

7 Make a series of small black dots on the cheeks and muzzle area, using the illustration as a guide. Spray again with fixative and leave to dry.

8 Cut out narrow strips of colored paper for the top of the mane, shaping them into a point at one end.

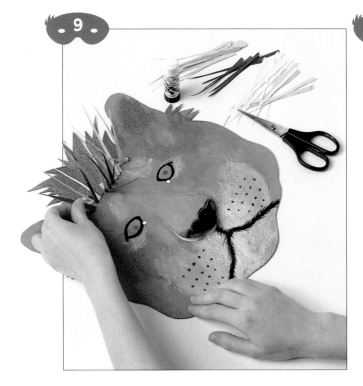

9 Begin to glue the strips to the top of the mask to create the shape of the head, adding strips of paper in different shades of brown and yellow.

10 Cut out some strips of white paper for the whiskers on the muzzle and chin and glue them in place.

11 Cut some longer strips for the side of the mane.

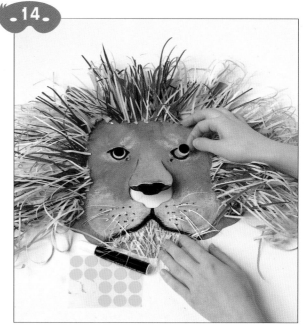

12 Cut some pieces for the mane from strips about 1 inch wide. Do not cut all the way along the strips, but roll them up at the uncut end and glue them in place at the sides.

13 When the glue is dry, carefully run some of the strips of paper between the edge of the blade of a pair of scissors and your thumb to curl the paper slightly.

14 Put a black self-adhesive dot on a larger yellow dot for each eye, and press them into position.

MEDUSA MASK

This mask is based on the legend of Medusa, a monster in Greek mythology whose hair was a mass of living snakes. This cardboard and paper mask requires a little patience to make, and you will also need to exercise your painting skills in decorating the face and applying the hair.

You will need

◊ Lightweight cardboard
◊ Pencil
◊ Tracing paper
◊ Craft knife
◊ Scissors
◊ Clear, all-purpose glue
◊ Paints, including red, green, and yellow
◊ Toothbrush
◊ Large and small paintbrushes
◊ White paper
◊ Black paper
◊ Strong tape
◊ Self-adhesive dots
◊ Hole punch

1 Transfer the outlines of the masks from the templates on page 47 and cut them out carefully from the cardboard.

2 Use a craft knife to cut a slit in the mouth.

3 Cut along the lines indicated on the template and fold the top part of the mask into shape by overlapping the cut areas and gluing them together to create the three-dimensional effect.

4 Repeat with the lower section. Fold and glue the nose along the lines shown on the template. Do not attach it to the mask yet.

5 Fit the top section of the mask to the lower part and glue the two sections together. Leave to dry.

6 Mix some red paint and use an old toothbrush to spatter paint over the surface of the mask and the nose.

7 Mix green paint and repeat the process, this time using a large, soft paintbrush.

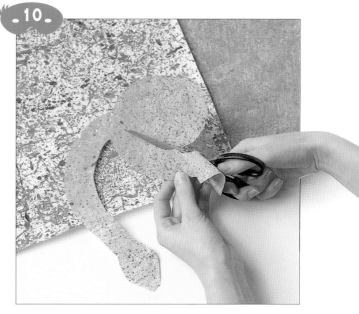

8 Mix some yellow paint and flick it over the mask and nose until you have built up a good covering of color.

9 Make as many snakes as you need from light-weight white paper. Draw a rough free-hand circle and mark the outline of the snake with a pencil, using the template as a guide. Decorate them with different patterns and colors to create a variety of textures.

10 Cut out the snakes, using your pencil line as a guide, but do not make them all exactly the same.

11 Begin to glue the cut-out snakes to the front of the mask, twining them together to make them look as if they are alive. Try to not to put snakes that are the same color next to each other, and leave a few heads and tails visible.

12 Use a fine paintbrush and white paint to add some final details to the snakes' heads and then paint in Medusa's eyebrows and the snakes' eyes in black or brown.

13 Paint in Medusa's mouth with dark red.

14 Cut out some small strips of black paper in the shape of snakes' tongues and glue them to the snakes' heads.

15 Position the nose, securing it at the back of the mask with strong tape.

16 Punch a hole in the center of a self-adhesive dot. Fit the dot into the eye hole, pressing it down firmly into place. Repeat for the other eye.

WOODLAND
HALF-MASK

This is the perfect mask for someone who enjoys walking in the countryside and picking up odd bits and pieces. The base is made of papier-mâché, molded on modeling clay, and it is decorated with leaves and berries. It is rather delicate, so handle it with care. Make sure that you use good-quality gold, bronze, and silver paints to give it a really sumptuous look.

You will need
◊ Pencil
◊ Tracing paper
◊ Lightweight cardboard
◊ Modeling clay
◊ Newspaper and paste for papier-mâché
◊ Craft knife
◊ Scissors
◊ Elastic
◊ Gold, silver, and bronze spray paint
◊ Selection of dry leaves, berries, fruit, and so on
◊ Clear, all-purpose glue

TIP
• If you do not like working with papier-mâché or you do not have the time that is needed to model the mask, try decorating the basic shape of the Feathered Half-mask on page 26 –but remember to omit the beak.

1 Trace the template on page 45 and transfer the image to a piece of cardboard.

2 Use modeling clay to mold the shape on the cardboard. Begin to build up a three-dimensional shape around the nose area, smoothing and refining the shape out toward the eyes.

3 Use the palms of your hands to smooth the clay and the edges.

4 Take special care to shape the nose and to smooth the clay around it, then leave the mold to dry for 24 hours.

5

5 Mix the paste to an even consistency and use torn scraps of newspaper, dipped in the paste, to cover the clay with a layer of papier-mâché. Squeeze the strips with your fingers to remove excess paste from the paper before you press it in place or the papier-mâché will take too long to dry.

6

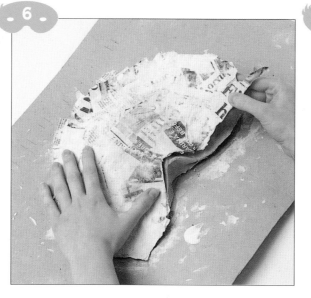

6 Leave the mask in a warm place for 2–3 hours to dry, then repeat the process three more times – that is, you will apply a total of four layers of papier-mâché. Leave the mask to dry completely, preferably overnight, before removing the mask from the mold.

7

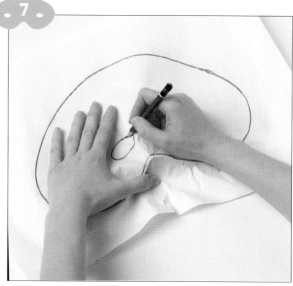

7 Using the template as a guide, draw eye holes on the mask and cut them out carefully with a craft knife.

8

9

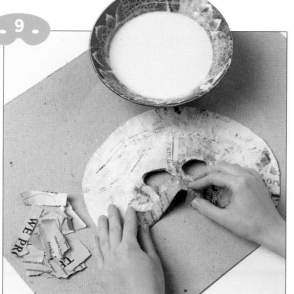

8 Trim the rough edges of the mask with scissors.

9 Use small pieces of papier-mâché all around the edge to finish it and to make a smooth line.

10 Make a small hole at each side and, from the back, push through the elastic, securing the ends with small knots.

10

11 Cover your work surface with newspaper, or work outside and spray the mask evenly with gold paint.

12 Spray the leaves, berries, nuts, and fruit with gold, silver, or bronze paint and leave them to dry.

13 Begin to glue the leaves over the mask, using different colors and shapes to build up the overall shape. Finish off by adding the fruits, nuts, and berries.

TIPS

• When you use spray paints, always work in a well-ventilated room – better still, work outside. You might prefer to use metallic paints that are applied by brush.

• Leaves should be preserved between paper and weighted down with books for one to two weeks before use.

PANDA

Fur fabric is ideal for animal masks – they always look so appealing. You can buy fur fabric in most fabric and craft stores, and it is easy to work with. The panda is very straightforward to make, and you could easily adapt the basic method to make almost any type of animal you want.

You will need
◊ Pencil
◊ Tracing paper
◊ Lightweight white cardboard
◊ Scissors
◊ Hole punch
◊ Fur fabric, white and black
◊ Clear, all-purpose glue
◊ White pencil or chalk
◊ Small, shallow yogurt container
◊ Buttons for eyes and nostrils

1 Transfer the outline from the template on page 46 to white cardboard and cut it out.

2 Cut out the nose and punch out the eye holes.

3 Trace around the cardboard template onto the reverse side of the white fur fabric, but do not trace around the ears.

4 Cut out the outline of the head and cut out the nose hole.

5 Glue white fur fabric onto the cardboard template and leave the glue to dry.

6 Pierce the eye hole with the sharp points of your scissors. Make sure you can see through the holes. You may have to trim some of the fur on the right side of the mask so that you can see clearly.

7 Cut out the templates for the ears, eye patches, and nose, and draw them on the reverse side of the black fabric.

8 Cut the ears, eyes, and nose patch from the black fabric.

9 Cut out the snout template and cut a piece of white fur fabric to size. Glue it around the yogurt container, making a triangular shape for the nose patch (see step 11).

11 Glue the black nose piece, reverse side up, onto the end of the yogurt container.

10 Tuck the extra bits of white fur fabric into the yogurt container and glue them in position.

12 Glue the eye and ear patches to the main mask. Make sure that you join the edges of the black and white neatly together.

13 Glue the nose into the middle of the mask between the black eye patches.

14 Glue buttons in position for the eyes and nostrils and leave until the glue is dry.

FEATHERED HALF-MASK

This feathered half-mask is quite sophisticated, and it would look great with an evening dress. Feathers always make a mask look elegant and exotic, but they are easy and quick to use. Although we have used green and black feathers, you can buy dyed ones and, by changing the basic shape of the mask, you could make a parrot or a peacock or an owl – or almost anything else you wanted. You can also mount this kind of mask on a stick in case you do not want to wear it all evening.

You will need
◊ Black cardboard
◊ Tracing paper
◊ Pencil
◊ White pencil or crayon
◊ Scissors
◊ Craft knife
◊ Clear, all-purpose glue
◊ Wooden toothpick
◊ Sequins
◊ Feathers, green and black
◊ Strong tape
◊ Black twill tape for tying

TIP

• Sequins can be fiddly to position. Look out for the kind that are sold stitched together in long strings. These are much easier than loose ones to attach in a straight line.

1 Draw the template image on page 46 onto tracing paper and go over the outline with a white pencil. Transfer this image to black cardboard by pressing down firmly on the wrong side of the pencil line. The image should be clearly visible on the board.

2 Cut out the mask and the two pieces of beak from the cardboard. Score lightly along the length of the upper edge of both beak sections.

3 Cut a series of small incisions along the top edge of the beak, taking care that you do not cut beyond the score line. Bend along the score line carefully.

4 Apply a line of glue to the cut edges and press the two pieces together firmly to make the beak.

5 Decorate both sides of the edge of the beak with gold heart-shaped sequins. Use a toothpick to help you position the sequins in an even line.

6 Glue the beak in position between the eye holes. Wait until the glue is dry. You may have to hold the beak in place for a few minutes until it is securely held in position.

7 Begin to glue the feathers around the mask, starting in the center and working out to the side. Try to make the two sides as symmetrical as possible.

8 Turn the mask over and use strong tape to hold black twill tape near the eye holes.

- 9 -

- 10 -

9 On the right side, use glue and the toothpick to stick multicolored heart-shaped sequins onto the feathers.

10 Finish the mask by gluing a line of gold sequins around each eye hole.

SANTA CLAUS

Paper plates make good bases for masks – they are cheap, readily available, and easy to use.
You could use the same method to make a pumpkin for a Halloween party or a snowman
for a Christmas party, or a rag doll, a scarecrow, a football or even a clock. Even fairly young
children can use this method, and you can use all kinds of different things to decorate
them – so save all your odd scraps of material, beads, straw, and felt.

You will need
◊ 4 large paper plates
◊ Pencil
◊ Ruler
◊ Scissors
◊ Hole punch
◊ Craft knife
◊ Paints
◊ Large and small paintbrushes
◊ Self-adhesive dots
◊ Clear, all-purpose glue

1 Use the template on page 48 and draw the nose and eye holes on a large paper plate. Punch out the eye holes and cut out the nose.

2 Cut out the separate nose section, fold it in half down the center and paint it pink. Use the same paint to color the plate pink. Draw two circles for the cheeks, and color two self-adhesive dots with blue paint for the eyes.

3 Punch a hole in the middle of the self-adhesive dots and position them over the eye holes. Paint the cheeks red.

4 Glue the nose in position between the cheeks.

5 Using the template and illustrations as reference, cut the hair and moustache from a paper plate.

6 Cut the beard from another plate, making the separate strands as fine and even as you can.

7 Glue the fringe and moustache into place on the face, holding them until the glue is dry.

8 Glue the beard in place.

9 Glue on the hair in sections. There are three sections at each side, so begin with the lowest one, making sure they are placed symmetrically.

10 Cut out the hat and paint it red.

11 Cut out the semicircle for the decorative band on the hat and glue it into place.

12 Glue the hat onto the main mask, holding it in place until the glue is dry.

13 Decorate the hat with self-adhesive white dots.

WITCH

This is a traditional papier-mâché mask, made on a balloon, which is one of the easiest and best ways of making a mask for a complete costume. It is the perfect mask for Halloween or for a costume party. Although it is time-consuming to make, it offers great scope for you to use your imagination, both in making the facial features and in adding decorations to the hat.

You will need

◊ Balloon
◊ Newspaper and paste for papier-mâché
◊ Modeling clay
◊ Craft knife
◊ Scissors
◊ Black crayon or pencil
◊ Paints
◊ Large and small paintbrushes
◊ Twill tape for ties
◊ Pencil or white crayon
◊ Length of string
◊ Thumbtack
◊ Heavy- or medium-weight black cardboard
◊ Double-sided tape or clear, all-purpose glue
◊ Black raffia
◊ Strong tape
◊ Plastic lizards, newts, spiders, etc.
◊ Silver net

1 Blow up the balloon to slightly larger than your head. Tear some newspaper into strips and dip the pieces into the paste, squeezing off the excess with your fingers. Cover about three-quarters of the balloon with pasted paper and leave it to dry.

2 Repeat the process twice more – that is, you apply three coats of papier-mâché in all – and leave it to dry completely. Burst the balloon, remove the pieces and trim off the edges of the papier mâché.

3 Use modeling clay to mold a nose. Add some small round balls to represent warts.

4 Tear some more, smaller strips of newspaper and cover the nose with papier-mâché. Leave to dry. Apply another layer of papier-mâché and leave to dry.

5 Cut the nose in half with a craft knife. Carefully peel off the nose from the clay, taking care that it does not tear.

6 Join the two halves of the papier-mâché nose with small pieces of pasted paper.

7 Trim the edges of the nose carefully with scissors so that it will sit securely on the front of the mask.

8 Place the nose in the center of the mask and hold it in place with small pieces of papier-mâché. Leave it to dry.

9 Draw on the face, eyebrows, cheeks, and mouth with black pencil.

TIP

• When you make papier-mâché, tear the paper so that you do not have sharp, cut edges, which do not lie smoothly, and always tear the strips in the same direction.

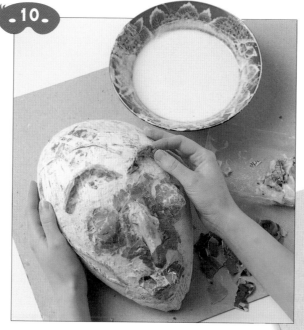

10 Make a small amount of papier-mâché pulp (see page 6) and build up the eyebrows, cheeks, and chin. Leave to dry overnight.

11 Roll small pieces of newspaper and dip them in paste, gluing them on the mask to represent wrinkles and lines.

12 Paint the face all over with pale gray, making sure that you cover all the newsprint.

13 Use dark gray paint and a fine brush to paint all the wrinkles and lines.

14 Pierce the eye holes with the point of the scissors. Try on the mask at this stage to make sure you can see properly.

15 Begin painting the cheeks, nose, chin, eyes, and so on with red and pink paint.

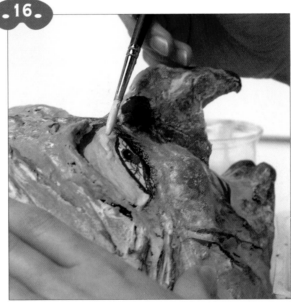

16 Use white to paint around the eyes and between the lips, and use dark red to paint the lips and warts and to outline the eyes. Make the eyes themselves look bloodshot by painting in fine red lines. Paint the area below the eyebrows with pale pink.

17 Use black paint for the eyebrows.

18 Pierce a hole on each side of the face with the point of your scissors. Push lengths of twill tape through the hole and knot it on the inside to hold it secure.

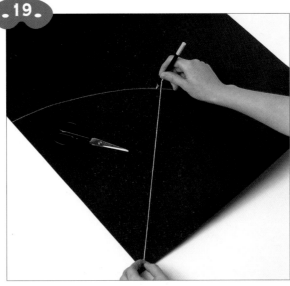

19 To make the hat, attach a piece of string to a pencil. Make a loop at the other end of the string and hold it in place with a thumbtack in the corner of the cardboard. Keeping the string taut, draw an arc on the cardboard that will make a cone large enough to make the witch's hat. Cut out the shape.

20 Use double-sided tape or glue to hold the long sides of the cone together.

21 Place the cone on a sheet of black cardboard and use a white crayon to draw around the base.

22 Decide how broad the brim should be, trying to keep it in proportion with the height of the hat and the features of the mask. Use a piece of paper, compasses, or a large plate to mark the edge of the brim and cut out the ring. Make a series of small cuts around the inside of the brim.

23 Fold the cuts upward and apply glue on the sides facing the rim.

24 Glue the crown of the hat onto the brim, making sure that the brim is firmly stuck to the crown.

25 Cut the black raffia to suitable lengths and use small pieces of tape to stick clumps of hair to the inside of the hat.

26 Glue the lizard, net, and spider to the hat and leave to dry.

PUNK

Papier-mâché masks always take a long time to make because you have to wait for the individual layers of pasted paper to dry. However, the results are so spectacular and impressive that it's always worth the effort. We decided to make this punk look fairly restrained and sculptural by applying a single color, but you could use a variety of colors to make the face look more – or less – sinister.

You will need
◊ Kitchen foil
◊ Scissors
◊ Newspaper and paste for papier-mâché
◊ White paint
◊ Paintbrush
◊ Tracing paper
◊ Pencil
◊ Lightweight white paper
◊ Clear, all-purpose glue
◊ Wire for earrings, nose rings, etc.
◊ Safety pins
◊ Chain, cross, or other decorations
◊ Twill tape for ties

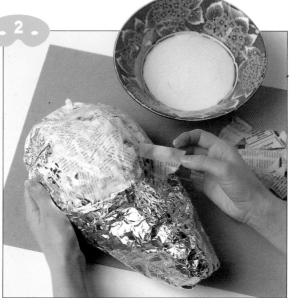

1 Take three sheets from a wide roll of kitchen foil and press them over your face so that you get a reasonable impression of your features. The mask will eventually fit under your chin and around over the top of your head, so make sure that you have enough foil to cover the whole area. You will need to press quite firmly around your nose, mouth, and eyes.

2 Mix the paste to a smooth, even consistency and tear strips of paper. Dip the strips into the paste, removing the excess paste with your fingers. Take great care when you apply the pasted paper to the foil that you do not press it out of shape. Apply one layer of paper and leave to dry for 2–3 hours. When the first layer is dry, apply three more layers – that is, there are four layers of papier-mâché in total – allowing each layer to dry before you apply the next.

3 Leave the final layer to dry overnight. When you are sure that the papier-mâché is completely dry, carefully pull the foil away from the inside.

4 Make a small amount of papier-mâché pulp (see page 6) and use it to build up the eyebrows and nose. Leave it to dry for at least 2 hours.

5 Roll small balls of papier-mâché pulp and use them for the eyeballs, positioning them carefully on the mask. Leave to dry.

6 Use more papier-mâché pulp for the lips, using the end of your scissors to shape them. Leave to dry.

7 When you are satisfied with the shape of the lips, begin to build up the ears. You may need to look at yourself in the mirror as you work to position and shape them correctly. Leave the mask in a warm, dry place until it is absolutely dry. This can take 24 hours because pulp often takes longer than ordinary papier-mâché to dry right through.

8 Make eye holes with the points of a pair of scissors; then hold the mask to your face to make sure that you can see through the holes. Make two holes at the base of the nose so that you can breathe when the mask is over your head. Also make the holes at the sides through which the twill tapes for tying will be attached.

9 Paint the entire mask with white. You may need to apply two coats to cover the newsprint completely – remember to allow the first coat of paint to dry before you apply the second.

10 Cut out triangles of white paper and roll them up to make the hair spikes. It can be difficult to get the paper to roll just as you want, but persevere and you will soon get the knack.

11 Apply some glue to the inside edge of the paper so that it does not start to uncurl. Do not use stiff paper, which will not roll easily and will be difficult to keep in shape.

12 You will need to have smaller spikes for the front of the head, with larger ones toward the back. Cut the spikes so that they decrease in size gradually.

13 Snip the ends of the spikes in three places and pull the paper out a little so that there is a larger surface for gluing.

14 Apply glue to the cut ends and press each spike firmly down on the top of the mask. You may need to hold each spike in place until the glue begins to dry.

15 Use a sharp pin or needle to pierce holes in the nose as well as the ears.

16 Make earrings and nose rings from garden wire and push them through the holes.

17 Push a safety pin through one side of the nose, and take the chain and cross from one side of the nose to the ear. Push a length of twill tape through the holes on each side and knot it on the inside to hold it securely.

MONSTER MASK

This enviro-monster is made from recycled egg boxes – you will need the molded cardboard kind, not the newer clear plastic containers, and you will need a lot, so begin to collect them now. This mask costs very little to make and it would be a good summer vacation project. The basic method could be used with all kinds of recycled containers – boxes, cartons, and even bottles – to make some really frightening monsters.

You will need
◊ Egg cartons
◊ Scissors
◊ Stapler
◊ Large and small styrofoam balls
◊ Clear, all-purpose glue
◊ Paint, including green, yellow, and red
◊ Large and small paintbrushes
◊ Florist's wire
◊ Pliers
◊ Self-adhesive dots
◊ Lightweight white paper
◊ Paste
◊ Newspaper
◊ Strong tape
◊ Red paper
◊ Strips of lightweight card

1 Separate the individual containers from the cartons – they should pull apart quite easily – then staple them together into the shape of a face.

2 Glue small styrofoam balls between the sections, especially if there are any holes. You can buy styrofoam balls in various sizes in craft and hobby stores. Remember to leave eye holes.

3 Mix a murky green and paint the mask all over. Leave to dry.

4 Mix some yellow paint and apply it to parts of the mask to create some interesting highlights – or to look like slime.

5 Take two large styrofoam balls and push a length of florist's wire (stub wires) into and through each ball. Florist's wire is available in craft stores and flower stores. Use pliers or your fingers to bend over the top of the wire; then pull the wire down so that the hook is caught securely in the top of the ball.

6 Hold the wires while you paint both balls yellow. Leave them to dry.

7 Mix some red paint and use a fine brush to paint red lines representing veins on the balls.

8 Paint two large self-adhesive dots with the same red and place them in the center of the balls, over the end of the wire hook.

9 Push the wires through the mask so that the eyes are positioned where you want them, then twist the wires around on the inside of the mask to hold the eyes securely. Cut off any excess wire and cover the cut ends with strong tape. Try on the mask to make sure that you can see through it.

10 Make some whiskers by tearing white paper into long strips. Twist the strips and dip them into the paste so that they will retain their shape. Leave them to dry.

11 When the paste is dry, paint the whiskers – we chose gray, but you can use any color you wish.

12 Use the points of your scissors to make a series of closely spaced, small holes at the sides of the mask. Thread the whiskers through the holes, adding a drop of glue to hold each one in place if you want to.

13 Make the fangs from strips of newspaper, twisted into shape and dipped into paste. You will probably find it easier to make the fangs nicely pointed when they have been dipped in the paste, and while they are wet, curve them slightly.

14 Leave the fangs to dry, then paint them, using the red and yellow paints to mix orange for the tips.

15 When the paint is dry, glue the fangs to a strip torn from an egg box, curving it slightly so that it fits along the bottom of the mask.

16 Use glue or tape to attach the row of fangs to the bottom inside edge of the mask.

17 Tear a tongue shape from red paper or color white paper with red paint.

18 Tape the tongue to the mask so that, from the front, it appears to be behind the fangs.

19 Staple strips of cardboard to the back of the mask, trying it on to make sure that the strips hold the mask securely but not too tightly over your face.

TEMPLATES

For reasons of space, the templates shown here are reproduced at half actual size. Before you can begin work, you will need to enlarge the outlines.

The easiest method of enlarging is, of course, by photocopying. Many libraries, stationery stores, and office equipment outlets have photocopiers with an enlargement facility. Even if the photocopier cannot make a direct enlargement to twice the original size, you can usually enlarge the enlargement until you have the necessary dimensions.

If you do not have access to a photocopier, use the grid method. Use a sharp pencil and a ruler to draw a series of equally spaced lines across and down the original template. Try to surround the curved edges with the edges of a square or rectangle so that the edges of the shape just touch the straight edges. Take a large, clean sheet of paper or cardboard and draw on it a square or rectangle that is twice as large as the original. Then cover this with vertical and horizontal lines that are spaced at

twice the distance of your first grid. For example, if the original squares were 1 inch on the original, you would draw squares of 2 inches. If the pattern is complicated, you will probably find it easier to have a small grid, say ½ inch, on the original and 1 inch on the enlarged version. Transfer the shapes that are visible in each small square to the corresponding larger square on the new grid. If necessary, go over the outlines with a black felt-tip pen.

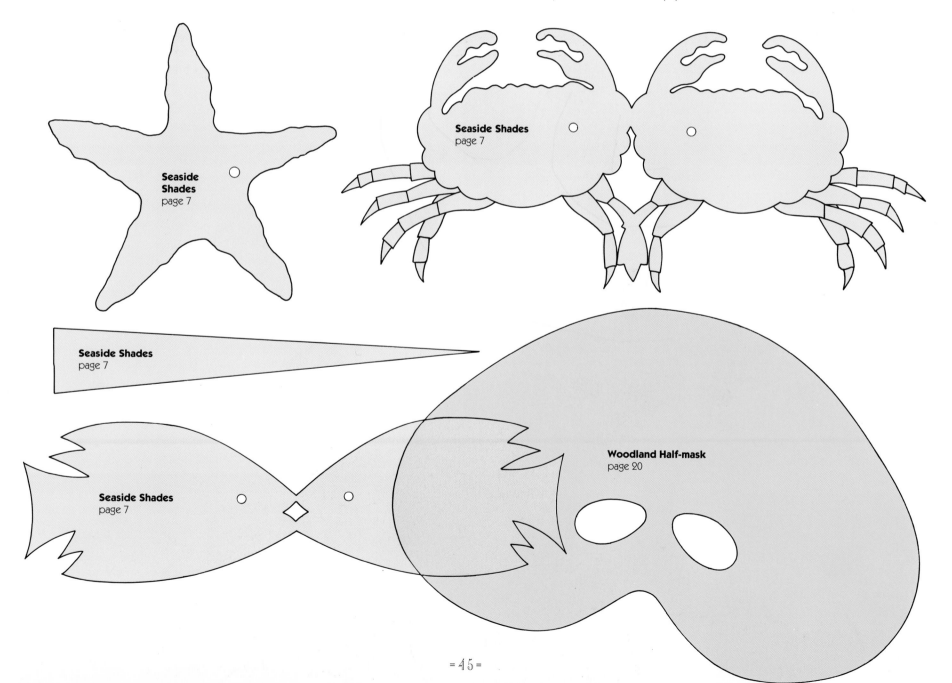

Seaside Shades
page 7

Seaside Shades
page 7

Seaside Shades
page 7

Seaside Shades
page 7

Woodland Half-mask
page 20

Panda
page 23

Panda
page 23

Panda
page 23

Feathered Half-mask
page 26

Half-mask (woman)
page 10

Feathered Half-mask
page 26

Feathered Half-mask
page 26

Lion Mask
page 13

Medusa Mask
page16

Medusa Mask
page16

Medusa Mask
page16

Medusa Mask
page16

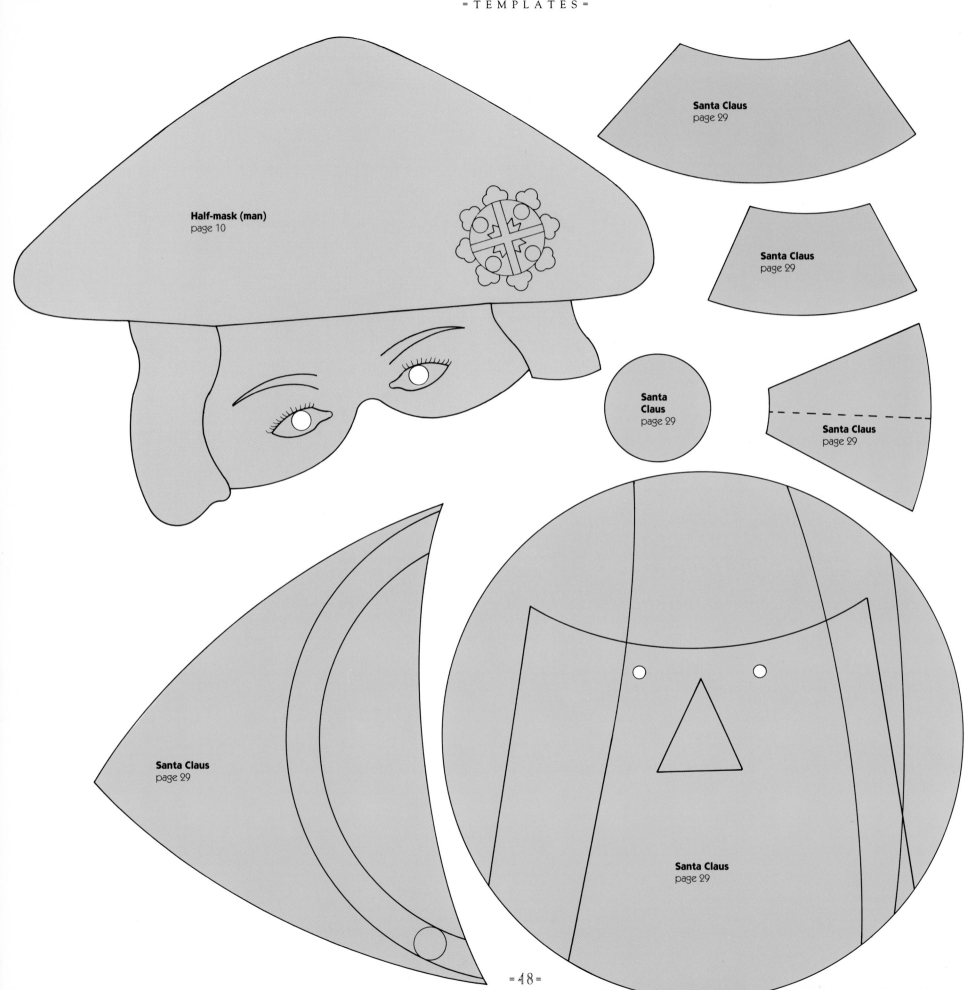

Santa Claus
page 29

Santa Claus
page 29

Half-mask (man)
page 10

Santa
Claus
page 29

Santa Claus
page 29

Santa Claus
page 29

Santa Claus
page 29